Animals in My Backyard
GOPHERS

Aaron Carr

www.av2books.com

LET'S READ
AV2
BY WEIGL™
ADDED VALUE • AUDIO VISUAL

Go to **www.av2books.com**, and enter this book's unique code.

BOOK CODE

G685868

AV² by Weigl brings you media enhanced books that support active learning.

AV² provides enriched content that supplements and complements this book. Weigl's AV² book strive to create inspired learning and engage young minds in a total learning experience.

Your AV² Media Enhanced books come alive with...

 Audio
Listen to sections of the book read aloud.

 Video
Watch informative video clips.

 Embedded Weblinks
Gain additional information for research.

 Try This!
Complete activities and hands-on experiments.

 Key Words
Study vocabulary, and complete a matching word activity.

 Quizzes
Test your knowledge.

 Slide Show
View images and captions, and prepare a presentation.

... and much, much more!

Published by AV² by Weigl.
350 5th Avenue, 59th Floor New York, NY 10118
Websites: www.av2books.com www.weigl.com

Library of Congress Cataloging-in-Publication Data
Carr, Aaron.
  Gophers / Aaron Carr.
    pages cm. -- (Animals in my backyard)
Includes index.
ISBN 978-1-4896-2946-3 (hard cover : alk. paper) -- ISBN 978-1-4896-2947-0 (soft cover : alk. paper) -- ISBN 978-1-4896-2948-7 (single user ebook)--
ISBN 978-1-4896-2949-4 (multi-user ebook)
1. Pocket gophers--Juvenile literature. I. Title.
QL737.R654C37 2014
599.35'99--dc23
                         2014040095

Printed in the United States of America in Brainerd, Minnesota
1 2 3 4 5 6 7 8 9 0 18 17 16 15 14

122014
WEP051214

Project Coordinator: Heather Kissock   Designer: Mandy Christiansen

Weigl acknowledges Getty Images, Alamy, Minden Pictures, and iStock as the primary image suppliers for this title.

Animals in My Backyard
GOPHERS

CONTENTS

Meet the gopher.

She is a small animal with a thick body and short legs.

She lives with her mother when she is young.

When she is young, she is blind and does not have any fur.

7

She has furry cheek pouches.

Furry cheek pouches let her store food to eat later.

She chews her food with her four long front teeth.

Her four long front teeth never stop growing.

Her front feet have sharp claws.

Sharp claws help her dig tunnels under the ground.

She can not see well in dark tunnels.

In dark tunnels, she uses her whiskers to find her way.

She eats mostly plant roots.

Plant roots give her the water she needs.

She can be found in North America and South America.

In North America and South America, she lives in places that have loose soil to dig.

If you meet the gopher,
she may be afraid.
She might run at you.

If you meet the gopher,
stay away.

20

21

GOPHER FACTS

These pages provide more detail about the interesting facts found in the book. They are intended to be used by adults as a learning support to help young readers round out their knowledge of each animal featured in the *Animals in My Backyard* series.

Pages 4–5

Gophers are small animals with thick bodies and short legs. There are about 38 species of gophers, all of which belong to the Rodentia order. Gophers range in size from about 5 to 14 inches (13 to 35 centimeters) in length. They weigh between 2 and 5 ounces (57 and 142 grams). A gopher's fur coat can be brown, yellow, black, or nearly white.

Pages 6–7

Gophers live with their mother when they are young. The babies are completely helpless when they are born. Their eyes and ears are closed, and they are hairless. The mother cares for her young for about six weeks. They usually leave the nest to live on their own after about two months.

Pages 8–9

Gophers have furry cheek pouches. Although they are commonly known as gophers, their proper name is "pocket gopher." This is a reference to their characteristic cheek pouches. Unlike other animals that carry food inside their cheeks, the gopher's fur-lined pouches are on the outside of its cheeks. The pouches can be turned inside-out for cleaning.

Pages 10–11

Gophers have four long front teeth that never stop growing. The gopher's front teeth, or incisors, can grow up to 14 inches (36 cm) in one year. These ever-growing teeth require constant chewing to keep them from growing too long. Gophers chew on tough foods, such as prickly pears, to help wear down their teeth.

Pages 12–13

Gophers have sharp claws. The gopher's front feet each have five toes, and each toe has a long, curved claw. These front claws are the gopher's primary digging tools. The back paws have much smaller claws that are mostly used for pushing debris out of the way. The gopher also uses its long front teeth to help dig.

Pages 14–15

Gophers cannot see well. With somewhat limited eyesight, gophers rely on their sensitive whiskers and tail to navigate their way around underground tunnels. Their whiskers feel the walls of the tunnel, which is usually about 4 inches (10 cm) wide. When running backwards, the gopher uses its tail like a whisker to feel the walls.

Pages 16–17

Gophers are plant-eaters, or herbivores. Although they will eat nearly any plant they come across, gophers most often eat roots, bulbs, and tubers. Sometimes, they eat roots they find while digging. Other times, they pull the entire plant into the tunnel to eat it. The plants have enough moisture in them that gophers do not need an open water source.

Pages 18–19

Gophers are found in North America and South America. Their range reaches from southern Canada to northern Colombia. Gophers make their homes in habitats ranging from prairies and grasslands to high mountain meadows above the timberline. They have been found living at elevations as high as 12,000 feet (3,658 meters).

Pages 20–21

Gophers and people often come into contact with each other. Most often, gophers will scurry back into their underground tunnels when they encounter people. However, gophers are known to bite if they feel threatened. Their bites can be very painful. People should give gophers plenty of space and consult the appropriate authorities if they become pests in the community.

KEY WORDS

Research has shown that as much as 65 percent of all written material published in English is made up of 300 words. These 300 words cannot be taught using pictures or learned by sounding them out. They must be recognized by sight. This book contains 51 common sight words to help young readers improve their reading fluency and comprehension. This book also teaches young readers several important content words. These words are paired with pictures to aid in learning and improve understanding.

Page	Sight Words First Appearance
4	the
5	a, and, animal, is, she, small, with
6	any, does, have, her, lives, mother, not, when, young
8	has
9	eat, food, later, let, to
10	four, long
11	never, stop
12	feet
13	help, under
14	can, in, see, well
15	find, way
16	give, needs, plant, water
18	be, found
19	places, that
20	at, away, if, may, might, run, you

Page	Content Words First Appearance
4	gopher
5	body, legs
6	blind, fur
8	cheek pouches
10	teeth
12	claws
13	ground, tunnels
15	whiskers
16	roots
18	North America, South America
19	soil

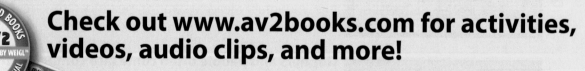

www.av2books.com